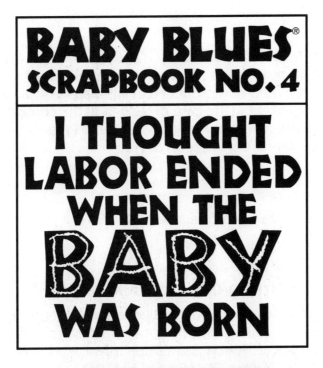

BABY BLUES®
SCRAPBOOK NO. 4

I THOUGHT LABOR ENDED WHEN THE BABY WAS BORN

BY **RICK KIRKMAN**
AND **JERRY SCOTT**

Andrews and McMeel
A Universal Press Syndicate Company
Kansas City

ISBN: 0-8362-1744-6

Library of Congress Catalog Card Number: 93-74269

First Printing, March 1994
Third Printing, August 1995

For Sukey—AH!

To Kim and Jerry—Welcome to the club

—*R.K.*

To Abbey

—*J.S.*

WORTHLESS OLD CATALOG.

EXPENSIVE COFFEE TABLE ART BOOK.

BABY.

HOW DO THEY KNOW??

EVIDENTLY IT'S THE SAME PHENOMENON THAT ATTRACTS TORNADOES TO TRAILER PARKS.

7

10

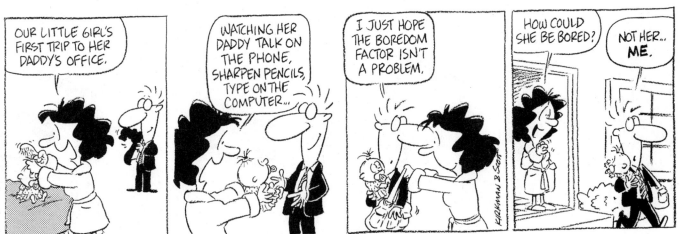

14

19

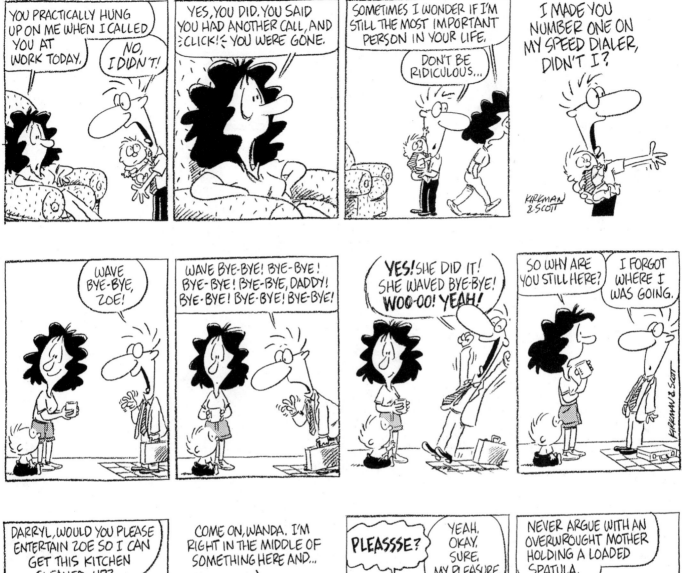

BABY BLUES®

BY RICK KIRKMAN / JERRY SCOTT

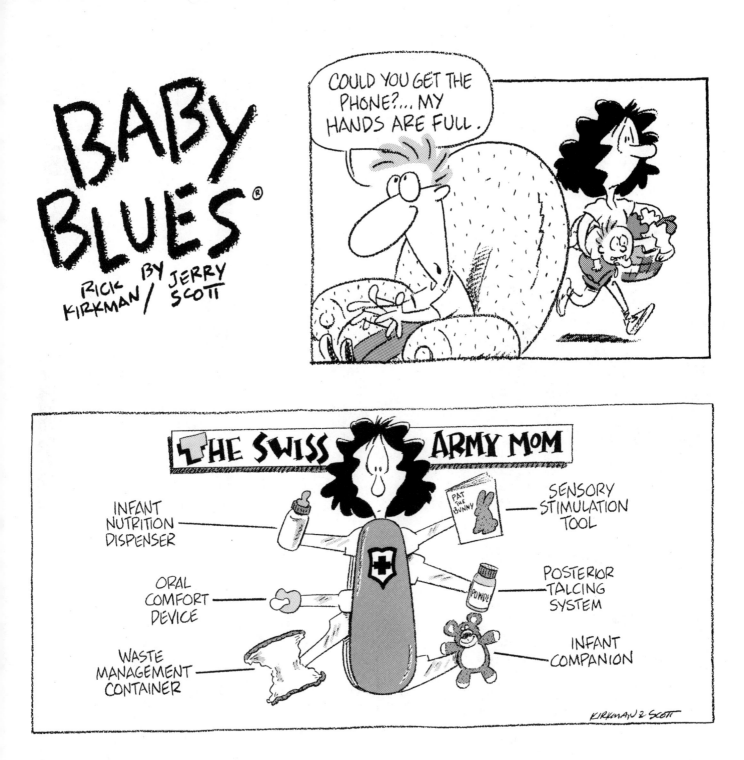

Panel 1: NO! ZOE! NO! NO! I WAS TAPING THAT SHOW! CLICK!

Panel 2: AAAAGH! NOT AGAIN!

Panel 3: MY WATCH! WHAM WHAM WHAM WHAM

KIRKMAN & SCOTT

Panel 4: ZOE'S FAVORITE GAME: "Let's Torment Daddy" I GIVE UP.

Panel 5: HI, MOM. LISTEN, YOU KNOW THAT ANTIQUE GRAVY BOAT THAT BELONGED TO YOUR GREAT AUNT HILDA?...IT BROKE. OH, NOOOO!

Panel 6: YEAH. IT JUST HAPPENED TODAY. I LO-O-O-VED THAT GRAVY BOAT!

Panel 7: IT'S IRREPLACEABLE! IT'S PRICELESS! IT WAS MY ONLY LINK TO MY GREAT AUNT HILDA! ZOE DID IT.

Panel 8: OH... WELL, IT WAS OLD ANYWAY. NO BIG DEAL. BYE!

KIRKMAN & SCOTT

Panel 9: DARRYL, ZOE'S MILK IS ALL GONE. CAN SHE HAVE A SIP OF YOURS? SURE.

Panel 10: SMACK! SLURP BLORBLE! BLORBLE! GRUNT!

Panel 11: GOODNESS GRACIOUS! YOU **WERE** THIRSTY WEREN'T YOU?

KIRKMAN & SCOTT

Panel 12: YOU'RE IN LUCK... SHE LEFT YOU A SIP. OF WHAT?

34

35

NOT BAD FOR A COUPLE OF NON-CAMPERS, IF YOU ASK ME.

THE CAMPSITE IS IN ORDER, THE TENT IS UP, THE FIRE IS BLAZING AND THE STEW WAS DELICIOUS.

NOW CAN WE GO HOME?

NO, IT'S NOT CAMPING UNLESS YOU SPEND THE NIGHT.

IS THAT GOOD? HMMM?

GIVE DADDY A KISS AND SAY "THANK YOU, DADDY!" "GIVE ME MORE!"

I THINK SHE'S HAD ENOUGH ROASTED MARSHMALLOWS, WANDA.

I'LL GET A WET-WIPE.

WELL, DINNER IS OVER AND THE DISHES ARE DONE...

CRACKLE CRACKLE

...I GUESS WE MAY AS WELL HIT THE SACK. WHAT TIME IS IT?

SEVEN FORTY-FIVE.

THAT'S ANOTHER THING I HATE ABOUT CAMPING — IT LASTS TOO LONG!

NO, WAIT... IT'S **SIX** FORTY-FIVE.

41

43

47

BABY BLUES®

BY RICK KIRKMAN / JERRY SCOTT

YOLANDA AND I WERE THINKING ABOUT BUYING A MINIVAN WHEN THE BABY IS BORN...

HOW DO YOU LIKE YOUR OXYMORON?

IT'S GREAT!

BUT IF YOU BUY ON, MIKE MAKE SURE YOU GET ONE EQUIPPED WITH THE FAMILY OPTION PACKAGE.

WHAT COMES WITH THAT? AIR BAGS? ANTI-LOCK BRAKES? BUILT-IN CHILD SEATS?

CENTRAL WET-WIPE DISPENSER.

OOH!

49

BABY BLUES®

RICK KIRKMAN / BY JERRY SCOTT

IS SHE ASLEEP?

I THINK SO.

SHE HAD A LONG NAP TODAY, SO I DON'T KNOW HOW LONG SHE'LL BE DOWN.

RIGHT. HERE'S THE LIST.

1. You look beautiful/sexy
2. Your hair is so soft
3. GRRRR!
4. MMM...What's that perfume
5. Hey, Big Boy, come to Mama
6. Kiss me, you fool
7. Your eyes are beautiful in this light
8. GIGGLE! GIGGLE! GIGGLE!
9. You're not so bad yourself
10. Hubba! Hubba!

LET'S SEE... NUMBER SIX, NUMBER EIGHT AND NUMBER FIVE...

WOW!

NUMBER TWO, NUMBER FOUR, NUMBER ONE, AND NUMBER TEN.

WHEN TIME IS OF THE ESSENCE...

I'M SORRY, DARRYL, BUT I CAN'T FORGIVE MYSELF THAT EASILY.

I SPANKED OUR BABY, SO I HAVE TO BE PUNISHED FOR IT...

...I'M PUTTING MYSELF IN TIME-OUT.

WHY DON'T YOU JUST GIVE YOURSELF A SPANKING?

TWO WRONGS DON'T MAKE A RIGHT!

KIRKMAN & SCOTT

KIRKMAN & SCOTT

COULD YOU TAKE OVER FOR A WHILE? HER FEET ARE KILLING ME.

NO, ZOE. YOU CAN'T STAND UP IN THE CART.

GRUNT! GRUNT!

I SAID, "NO!" NOW SIT DOWN.

UNH! UNH!

KIRKMAN & SCOTT

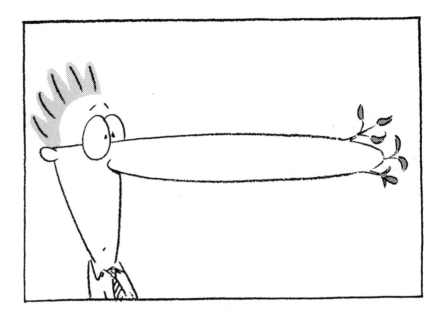

BABY BLUES®
BY RICK KIRKMAN / JERRY SCOTT

WELL, I GUESS THAT'S ABOUT IT, MOM.

THINGS ARE PR--

BA-ZING!

NAB!

ZIP!

--ETTY QUIET AROUND HERE.

THAT'S NICE.

KIRKMAN & SCOTT

71

BABY BLUES®
BY RICK KIRKMAN / JERRY SCOTT

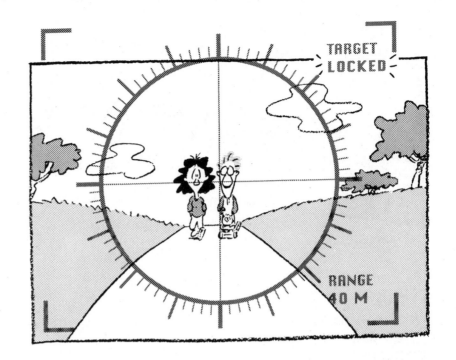

81

BABY BLUES®

BY RICK KIRKMAN / JERRY SCOTT

NOW SHOWING!
My Dinner with Zoe

IT SAYS HERE THAT IT HELPS A BABY'S LANGUAGE DEVELOPMENT IF YOU HOLD CONVERSATIONS WITH HER.

CONVERSATIONS??

YEAH...LIKE IF YOU ASK ZOE "HOW ARE YOU TODAY?," YOU'RE SUPPOSED TO WAIT FOR HER TO ANSWER.

OH?

HOW ARE YOU TODAY?

BODWEEMA...

DEEBABA WAPPA DOOBEEE AHHHHAHHHH POWOOW GOB GOB NUM NUMMA ZHABOW ZHA DOOMPEE NAM NAM WAHB NAHMA DABBO WEEEEEOOEEEOO

YOUR TURN.

I FORGOT WHAT WE WERE TALKING ABOUT!

KIRKMAN & SCOTT

Panel 1: NEXT, ON "MOTHERS AND BABIES," BAD HABITS YOU CAN PREVENT...

Panel 2: FIRST, THE PACIFIER SHOULD NOT BE USED BEYOND THE AGE OF TEN MONTHS.

POIT!

Panel 3: ALSO, AVOID IN-BETWEEN-MEAL SNACKS AND BOTTLES. RESERVE COMFORT TOYS FOR BEDTIME ONLY.

WHIP!

Panel 4: FOLLOWING THESE HELPFUL TIPS WILL ENSURE A MORE ENJOYABLE PARENTING EXPERIENCE.

WAAAAA!

Panel 5: BZZT CLICK!

Z Z

Panel 6: YAWN

WELL, WHAT DID YOU THINK?

KIRKMAN & SCOTT

Panel 7: I SLEPT LIKE A LOG THROUGH THE MIDDLE PART, BUT I KEPT WAKING UP DURING THE LAST PART.

ME, TOO.

Panel 8: REMEMBER WHEN WE USED TO ACTUALLY **SEE** THE MOVIES WE RENTED?

YAWN VAGUELY. LET'S CHECK ON THE BABY.

Panel 9: UP WE GO! UP WE GO! UP WE GO! UP WE GO! UP WE GO!

Panel 10: COME ON, YOU TWO... IT'S BEDTIME.

Panel 11: OH.

UH...

Panel 12: UP WE GO! UP WE GO! UP WE GO!

OOF!

KIRKMAN & SCOTT

89

93

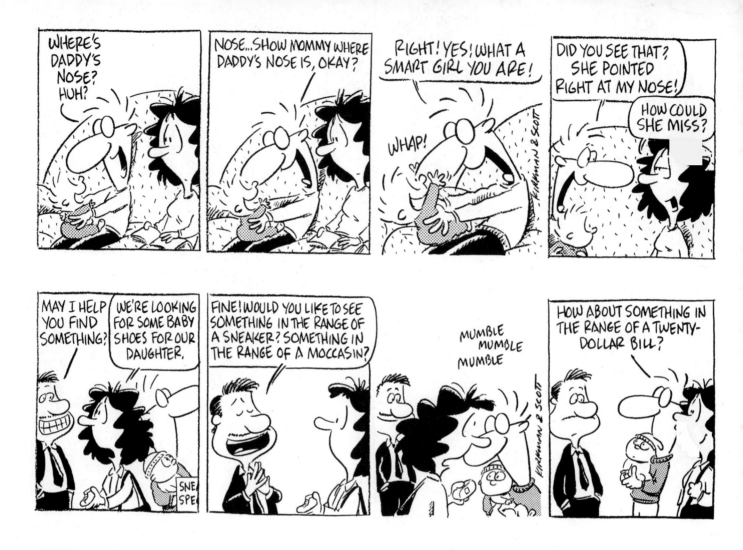

101

BABY BLUES®

RICK KIRKMAN / JERRY SCOTT

BABY BLUES

BY RICK KIRKMAN / JERRY SCOTT

110

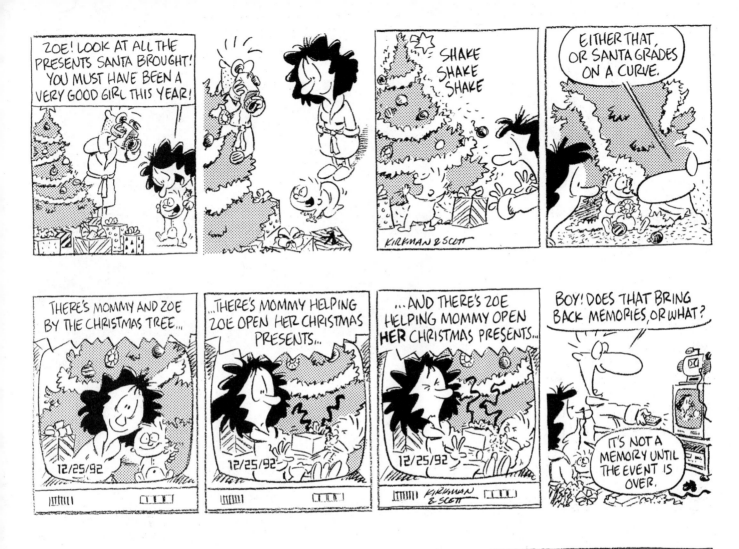

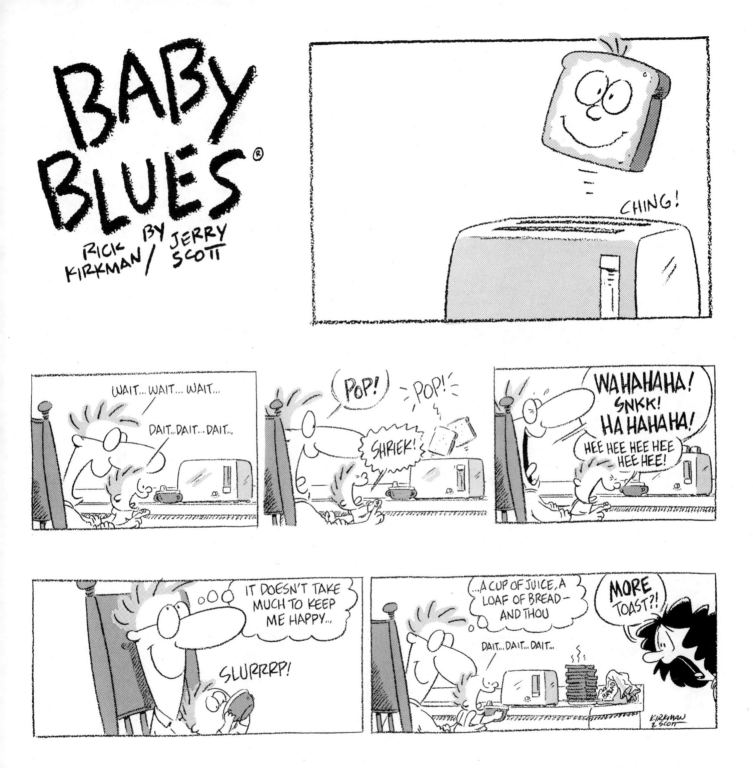

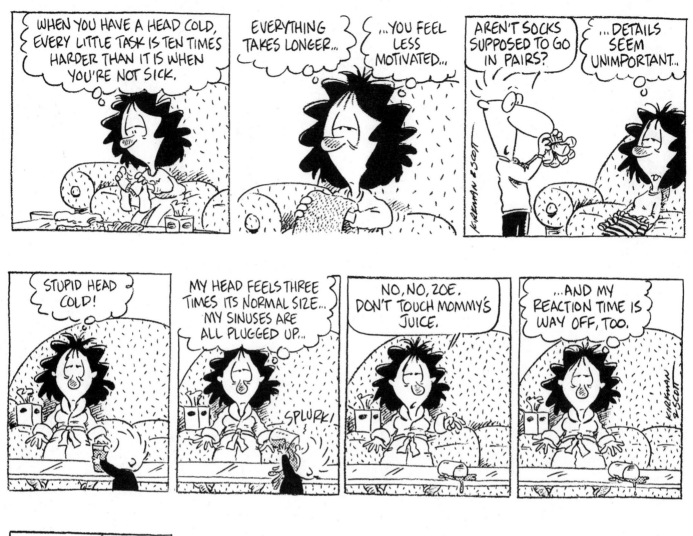

BABY BLUES®

BY RICK KIRKMAN / JERRY SCOTT

 WHERE ARE THE GUYS?

GUESS.

IT NEVER FAILS. WHENEVER YOU GET A FEW MEN TOGETHER, THEY ALWAYS END UP IN THE DRIVEWAY TALKING ABOUT CARS.

THEY'RE SO PREDICTABLE.

EQUIPMENT... PERFORMANCE... HANDLING... GADGETS... IT'S ALL THEY CAN EVER FIND TO TALK ABOUT!

...AND YOU OUGHT TO SEE HOW THIS THING CORNERS!

OOH!

YEAH, BUT WHAT ABOUT PAYLOAD?

PERSONALLY, I LIKE A SEPARATE COMPARTMENT FOR THE DIAPER BAG.

KIRKMAN & SCOTT